Original title:
Daffodil Dreams

Copyright © 2025 Creative Arts Management OÜ
All rights reserved.

Author: Mariana Leclair
ISBN HARDBACK: 978-1-80566-766-7
ISBN PAPERBACK: 978-1-80566-836-7

## The Dreamscape of Afternoon Light

In the sunlit noon, a flower grins,
With petals that tickle like playful pins.
Bees in a dance, doing their jig,
While ants complain, 'This is too big.'

A rabbit hops, wearing a hat,
Says, "Why so serious? Come, have a chat!"
The clouds overhead chuckle and swirl,
As the laughter of petals begins to twirl.

## A Garden of Whispered Wishes

In the garden, wishes take flight,
Chasing butterflies, what a sight!
Plants wearing smiles, so quite absurd,
Chatting away, not saying a word.

A snail races by, quite slow on grace,
In the race of dreams, he's lost his place.
With thorns laughing and roses in lull,
Each petal shares secrets, sweet and dull.

## Luminescent Visions of Spring

In springtime's glow, the buds all cheer,
Colorful blooms with nothing to fear.
A sunflower sings with a voice so bright,
'Who turned on the lights? It's a party tonight!'

A frog in a tie leaps onto a rock,
Announcing the show, 'What a great clock!'
With laughter echoing, the whole place beams,
As flowers sway, lost in their dreams.

## The Poetry of Verdant Landscapes

In hills of green, hiccups arise,
As grasshoppers jest, much to their surprise.
Each blade a pen, writing with flair,
A landscape of laughter fills the air.

The trees tell stories in whispers so sweet,
While daisies roll over, light on their feet.
With humor in roots and joy in each leaf,
Nature's a comedian, beyond belief.

## **Enchanted Moments in Blooms**

In the garden where giggles grow,
Butterflies dance with a silly show.
Bumblebees buzz with a comical hum,
All the flowers whisper, "Here we come!"

Petals in colors, a jester's delight,
Twisting and turning in the morning light.
They wear little hats, oh what a sight!
Swaying and laughing, all day and night.

## The Golden Hour of Blossoms

At twilight, the flowers throw a fest,
Each bloom dressed in yellow, looking its best.
They giggle and gossip, each petal a star,
"Have you seen Daisy? She's gone too far!"

The tulips are telling their best knock-knock,
While sunflowers stand as the watchful clock.
With jokes in the breeze, they lighten the air,
In this golden hour, laughter we share.

## Sunkissed Whispers of the Heart

In the warm glow where the petals tease,
They whisper sweet secrets on the soft breeze.
"Did you hear Geranium stole the show?"
"Shh, don't tell the roses, they're quite a show!"

With bees as the audience, buzzing away,
Every flower's a comedian, ready to play.
The sun gives a wink, the clouds giggle mild,
In this leafy theater, we're all just wild.

## A Tribute to the Sunlit Pastures

Pastures alive with a colorful scene,
Cows chuckle softly, they're part of the team.
The daisies are debating who's the fairest,
While the clovers cheer loud, giving their rarest.

A meadow recital, oh what a to-do!
Where every flower dons its brightest hue.
Laughter bursts forth from the land so grand,
In this sunlit theater, all hand in hand.

## The Dance of Yellow Hues

In the garden, yellow prancers,
They sway and whirl like tiny dancers.
A bumblebee in a tuxedo suit,
Spins around, with pollen loot.

With every gust, they bow and bend,
A floral party that won't quite end.
The sun bursts forth, they cheer and spin,
Join the fun, let the dance begin!

## Awakening in Verdant Fields

Waking up, a golden host,
Chasing after the sunlight's toast.
They giggle softly, in the breeze,
Inviting all to join with ease.

A squirrel trips in his acorn chase,
Falls right down, what a funny place!
The flowers chuckle, oh what a sight,
In this lush land, where all is bright!

## Beneath a Sky of Buttercups

Beneath the clouds of fluffy cream,
The blossoms burst, what a bright theme!
A mole pops up with a tiny cheer,
What a sight, not quite a deer!

They giggle as the rain drips down,
Wearing puddles like a crown.
These little suns, oh how they laugh,
Even the grass starts to do a gaffe!

## The Dawn of Floral Fantasies

As morning breaks with giggles bright,
Petals bounce for sheer delight.
A ladybug in a polka dot,
Thinks she's grand, gives quite a show jot.

The world awakes in silly blooms,
Each flower sharing secret tunes.
With carefree hearts, they paint the scene,
Life's a joke, and all's a dream!

## **Harmony of Blossoms and Whispers**

In a garden where the flowers play,
Bees wear tiny hats in a comical way.
Butterflies waltz on a swing made of air,
While ants line dance without a single care.

Chirpy voices from the leafy trees,
The squirrels gossip, sharing silly teas.
A daisy tells jokes, oh so spry,
While the sun chuckles, hanging in the sky.

## Sunlit Journeys through Flora

A picnic blanket stretched, quite a sight,
With sandwiches dancing in pure delight.
Lemons wink, limes giggle, so round,
And the grass tickles toes on the ground.

A squirrel skates by on a tiny board,
While petals applaud, making everyone roar.
Frogs in tuxedos sing a bubbly tune,
As the sun sets, drawing dreams with a swoon.

## **Blooming Hopes in a Soft Breeze**

Blossoms gather for an afternoon chat,
While a lazy snail wears a top hat.
Petals throw confetti, creating a fuss,
As birds join in with a big feathered bus.

Jellybeans tumble from clouds high up,
While flowers sip nectar from a cream-filled cup.
The wind joins the laughter, spinning around,
Till everyone giggles and joy is found.

## **The Charm of Nature's Palette**

Crayons of nature splash colors so bright,
As laughter echoes through the warm sunlight.
Moonlight tickles the petals at night,
While fireflies waltz, bringing pure delight.

A cheeky robin plays peek-a-boo,
And daisies whisper their secrets too.
With grass tickling noses in a hurry,
The earth spins in giggles, never a worry.

## **Blossoms of Hope Unfurled**

In a garden where giggles bloom,
The flowers plot a silly zoom.
Waltzing bees with little hats,
Chasing butterflies like acrobats.

A squirrel sneaks a funny peek,
As blooms burst forth with quirky cheek.
They laugh and shout, 'Let's spread the cheer!'
While ants parade to make it clear.

## **Echoes of Nature's Lullaby**

A frog croaks tunes of joy and pride,
While crickets play at night, they hide.
Beneath the moon, the flowers sway,
In a soft tune, they dance and play.

A hedgehog sings with all his might,
But sounds more like a yawn at night.
The rustle and giggles fill the space,
In nature's choir, there's not a trace.

## The Dance of the Verdant Skirts

Tall grasses twirl, a lively crew,
With petals swaying, it's quite the view.
A sunflower spins a dizzy tale,
While beetles cheer, waving their ale.

They stomp and shuffle, a merry bunch,
As bunnies join for a lunchtime crunch.
The garden's a party, vibrant and free,
Where nature's fun is pure glee!

## Where Sunbeams Softly Tread

Sunbeams tickle each bud and bloom,
While shadows giggle, making room.
A breeze whispers jokes to the trees,
As flowers laugh in the teasing breeze.

Petals play hide and seek from the sun,
While ladybugs race, just for fun.
In this patch of laughter, life is bright,
Where every moment feels just right!

## Flashes of Yellow Amongst the Green

·

Little blooms in a vast parade,
Dancing under sunshine, unafraid.
They wiggle and giggle, oh so spry,
Waving at bees as they drift on by.

In a field where mischief takes flight,
A joyful sight that feels just right.
They whisper secrets to passing bees,
Hoping to snag a sweet summer tease.

**Cradled by the Earth's Embrace**


Huddled close in the softest bed,
With whispers of laughter, no worries bred.
Tickled by winds that skip and sway,
These little stars brighten the day.

They peek at clouds with curious eyes,
Playing tricks, oh what a surprise!
Eager to prank every stumbling ant,
As they twirl in a joyful chant.

**The Gentle Brush of a Summer Whisper**

A breeze drifts by with a heartfelt giggle,
While petals perform their wiggly jiggle.
They share a joke with the fluttering bee,
 Ensuring all creatures sing with glee.

Like jesters adorned in golden threads,
In gardens where laughter never dreads.
They toss their heads in a playful cheer,
 Making all woes simply disappear.

## Beneath the Softest Sky

Under a canvas so plush and blue,
Little ones bloom, bringing joy anew.
They stretch to the sun with a silly grin,
Ready to welcome the fun to begin.

The clouds play peek-a-boo all day long,
As they join in on the vibrant song.
With laughter echoing from leaf to leaf,
They turn the mundane into sheer belief.

## The Golden Symphony of Renewal

In fields of gold, the seekers leap,
Chasing sunbeams, laughter deep.
With petals bright, they twirl and sway,
Their funny antics steal the day.

A bumblebee, quite out of tune,
Waltzes madly 'neath the moon.
His tiny legs, they twist and turn,
As rivals watch, they laugh and yearn.

## Blooming Sophistication in the Mist

A posh parade of blooms so fine,
In velvet hues, they sip on wine.
A tulip dons a sassy hat,
While daisies giggle at the cat.

The mist rolls in, quite suave and bright,
Yet grasshoppers dance, a silly sight.
In fancy shoes, they leap and glide,
Creating joy with every stride.

## **Luminous Journeys Through Green**

A gaggle of frogs, on lily pads,
Hold court with jokes that make you glad.
With winks and croaks, they spin their tales,
While dragonflies just roll their sails.

In patches lush, bugs play charades,
Dressed in hues of leafy shades.
A journey bright, with laughter spry,
As clouds drift by in cotton sky.

## The Harmonious Chorus of Spring

The birds assemble, a quirky band,
With melodies that twist and strand.
They chirp a tune, off-key but bold,
While rabbits dance, or so I'm told.

A hiccup here, a flap there too,
As nature laughs, as if on cue.
A symphony of giggles, sweet,
A silly song, no one can beat.

## **Canvas of the Gentle Dawn**

In morning's light, a canvas wide,
Colors splash like children hide.
The sun peeks over the hilltop's edge,
Painting shadows with a playful pledge.

Breezes tickle the flower's face,
While bees engage in a buzzing race.
The worms debate which way to wriggle,
While squirrels crack jokes and start to giggle.

Pollen flies with a sneeze so loud,
The sneezing flowers attract a crowd.
Nature laughs in shades so bright,
As petals dance in sheer delight.

With laughter woven through each hue,
Spring's canvas is a wacky view.
Join the revelry, join the cheer,
For laughter blooms as spring draws near.

## Where Dreams Meet Nature's Palette

A brush held firm by roots of grass,
Strokes of whimsy in a bright bold class.
The clouds giggle, they twist and swirl,
While paintbrush trees in beauty twirl.

Puddles form like mirrors wide,
Reflecting giggles from the sky's slide.
Nature's palette spills on the ground,
With pastel hues where fun is found.

Butterflies wear polka dot wings,
Dance antics of silly little things.
Each petal whispers a comic sigh,
As bees buzz tales that make you fly.

The sun throws beams with playful grace,
As laughter dots the landscape's face.
In this artful wild, join the spree,
Where dreams bloom wildly, wild and free.

## The Unraveling of Springtime Knots

Knotty branches stretch and yawn,
As nature wakes to a playful dawn.
Tangles of vines in hilarious glee,
Whispering secrets beneath the tree.

Budding jokes in every nook,
The squirrels share tales, come take a look.
A rabbit hops, with feet so fleet,
While making a prank dash down the street.

Petals fall with awkward grace,
Landing on faces in a funny place.
The wind trip-trods through the blooming heap,
Leaving behind a giggle and a peep.

Spring's pranks blossom, what a view,
With laughter sewn in every hue.
Join the fun, unwind the plight,
In nature's folly, there's sheer delight.

## Seeds of Joy Beneath the Snow

Under the snow, seeds whisper low,
Dreams of spring in frosty glow.
Laughing, they wiggle to shake off the chill,
Waiting for warmth with a quirky thrill.

Snowflakes dance like clowns on high,
Tickling the ground as they drift and vie.
While beneath, the seeds chuckle in sleep,
Planning the parties they'll soon keep.

When thaw comes knocking, it's time to rise,
Bursting forth in a playful surprise.
With colors bright and laughter loud,
Joy springs forth, making nature proud.

So here we await, with laughter in tow,
For warmth will bring a colorful show.
Beneath winter's cloak, hidden delight,
Seeds of joy wait for spring's invite.

## A Journey Through Blazing Meadows

In meadows bright, where flowers twirl,
The bees all dance, and petals swirl.
I tripped on clover, what a sight!
A rabbit laughed, then took to flight.

The sunbeam tickles, warms my nose,
A ladybug in polished clothes.
She stole my snack, oh what a thief!
Yet I can't stay mad; it's too brief.

A gust of wind, a silly chase,
Petals flew high, like they're in a race.
I lost my hat, it's off I go,
To retrieve it back, my bumpy show.

The meadow laughs in colors bright,
Each bloom winks, "Come play tonight!"
With every stumble, every cheer,
I revel in this joyful sphere.

## Sunlight's Serenade in Bloom

The sun's a jester, spinning round,
Daffodils giggle, making a sound.
A squirrel juggles acorns with flair,
I clap my hands, 'What's going on there?'

Butterflies flirt in colorful gowns,
While daisies gossip without any frowns.
A snail slips by, moving so slow,
He should join a race, let's give it a go!

Sunlight giggles, a warm embrace,
While tulips pout, they want some space.
The wind whispers secrets, soft as a tune,
Telling the flowers to dance 'neath the moon.

Each blossom laughs under sky's dome,
A floral party, in nature's home.
We'll find joy in each silly glance,
Join the garden; oh, let's dance!

## Blooms that Whisper of Promise

In a garden bright, whispers float,
Tulips gossip in flowered coats.
A bumblebee buzzes, oh so vain,
"My honey's sweet, it beats that grain!"

The sun peeks out, a grin on its face,
Not a shy star in this lively place.
The grass tickles toes, a soft, sly tease,
As daisies laugh in the playful breeze.

Lions of flowers with colors bold,
Boys with wild hats and stories told.
A petal slips, oh what a fall!
"Let's not let gravity take us all!"

Each bud's a giddy little sprite,
Making promises in broad daylight.
Let's dance around in this joyful bliss,
Chasing dreams, oh, what a twist!

## The Radiant Hearts of Spring

Beneath the sun, a bright parade,
Petals popping, nature's charade.
A dandy bee lost his way anew,
Claiming, "Excuse me, I'm part of the crew!"

The tulip crew strikes a pose so grand,
With colors so silly, you won't quite stand.
A carrot sneezes, it's quite absurd,
"Bless you!" they say, but not a word!

A worm with sunglasses, chilling low,
Says, "Come on now, let's take it slow!"
Laughter bubbles as flowers sway,
Who knew spring could be this way?

As laughter blooms and mischief spreads,
The blooms play hopscotch on flowerbeds.
In every petal, pure mirth takes root,
Let's celebrate spring, it's cute!

**Fields of Light and Laughter**

Golden blooms bounce in the breeze,
Wearing party hats like bees.
They giggle under rays so bright,
Whispering jokes all day and night.

With petals soft, they wiggle and swirl,
Like tiny dancers in a whirl.
Sunshine laughs, oh what a show,
These flowers steal the scene, you know!

## **Illuminated Dreams Beneath the Sky**

In fields where sunshine jumps with glee,
Flowers claim the best seat, you see!
They whisper secrets to the clouds,
While giggling softly, oh so loud.

Each petal glows with sunny cheer,
A bouquet of joy, oh dear, oh dear!
They throw a party, flowers unite,
Beneath the sky, oh what a sight!

## A Symphony of Yellow Florets

Tickled by the breeze, they sway,
Composing tunes in a joyful play.
Yellow notes dance with delight,
Singing praises to the light.

They form a band, all in a row,
Playing beats, putting on a show.
A melody of mischief and fun,
In this sunny garden, everyone!

## **Petal-Painted Reveries**

Oh, the petals wear colors so bright,
Creating visions that tickle the night.
Each bloom tells tales, with a twinkle and laugh,
Painting dreams upon sun's warm half.

Tripping over roots, they tumble and roll,
Nature's pranksters, filled with soul.
In a world where laughter truly beams,
Watch as they dance in our silliest dreams!

## **A Ballet of Blooming Dreams**

In the garden where giggles play,
Flowers dance in bright ballet.
Petals pirouette, twirling free,
A hilarious show for you and me.

Worms in tuxedos crawl with flair,
Squirrels try to join, but who would dare?
The daisies laugh, they can't be beat,
As rabbits hop to the funky beat.

## Whispered Sunshine in the Breeze

Sunshine whispers, a silly tune,
Buzzing bees play the kazoo in June.
Butterflies giggle as they glide,
Tickled by breezes, full of pride.

A ladybug winks, striking a pose,
While grasshoppers strike a dance with their toes.
The flowers chime in with a soft sigh,
"Let's party all day! Oh me, oh my!"

**Fields of Gold and Heartfelt Wishes**

Golden fields swaying with laughs,
Wishes float like happy gaffs.
Each bloom has a secret to share,
Stories of joy danced in the air.

A goat jumps high, trying to fly,
With dreams of landing in a pie!
The sun rolls its eyes, chuckling bright,
As petals giggle in pure delight.

## In the Embrace of Spring's Glow

Spring's hug is warm, filled with cheer,
Even the frogs croak songs of beer.
With every hop, they wear a crown,
Ribbits echo, never a frown.

Tulips and jests play hide and seek,
With every blush, they spring a peek.
The sun grins wide, joy in its rays,
Memories made in goofy displays.

## Kaleidoscope of Garden Fantasies

In a garden where gnomes dance,
Flowers giggle at every glance.
Twirling bees in tiny shoes,
Even the snails have funky moves.

Bumblebees wear tiny hats,
Laughing birds engage in chats.
The sun winks at the daisies' cheer,
As butterflies flutter with no fear.

Ladybugs play hide and seek,
While garden monsters sneak a peek.
Rabbits in sunglasses hop around,
In this whimsical playground.

Glowing bugs have a disco night,
Turning garden paths into pure delight.
With paintbrush flowers in every hue,
Nature's jesters make dreams come true.

## Petal Pathways to Tomorrow's Light

On the paths of colorful cheer,
Spinach jokes marinate near,
Radishes chuckle and turn pink,
Things get silly; just stop and think.

In the melon sings a replay,
Of fruit punch parties gone astray.
Carrots rock in their orange pants,
While onions ponder their life's dance.

With whimsical worms like poets' pens,
They scribble tales of garden friends.
Sun-kissed tomatoes wear a crown,
"Let's grow laughter, not a frown!"

In this cheerfully blooming space,
There's always room for just one face.
Where every petal spins a tale,
Of laughter dancing on the gale.

## Whispered Blooms of Spring

In a field of whispers, daisies conspire,
To tickle the clouds, lift spirits higher.
Tulips wear glasses, all chic and neat,
And gossip like girls in dazzling heat.

"Have you seen the roses' new hairdo?"
"Yeah, it's wild, but still quite cute!"
The violets laugh, rolling on grass,
While the lilies prance, letting time pass.

The daisy chain folks form a line,
Trading gooey laughter over sunshine.
Bees in tutus dance 'round with glee,
No one could guess what this wildness could be.

Life's a joke in this blooming show,
With petals about, laughter in tow.
Whispers of spring make for fun, you see,
Where flowers tell jokes in joyous spree.

## Golden Petals and Sunlight

In sunlight's arms, petals gleam,
They cozy up, living the dream.
A sunflower's hat is a sight quite bold,
Trading tales of wonders, laughing, uncontrolled.

"Nobody's taller," said the tall poppy,
While marigolds bicker, feeling snappy.
Petals sway, with giggles abound,
Where ecstasy in sunshine is found.

With bumblebees buzzing in funky form,
Ridiculous antics become the norm.
Blossoms tumble, twirl, and sway,
Join in the sunshine's playful ballet.

Golden petals in contagious delight,
Sharing secrets from morning till night.
In this garden, laughter is prime,
Where every bloom can have a good time.

## Chalice of the Springtime Sun

In a cup of yellow cheer,
The sun's a jester, never drear.
Flowers dance in silly ways,
Making honey from their praise.

Buzzing bees in tiny suits,
Polishing their flowery boots.
They giggle as they tip and twirl,
Spreading joy with every whirl.

The grass wears a ticklish grin,
While squirrels join in on the spin.
With every hop and wheely spin,
Nature's laughter does begin.

So raise your cups to springtime fun,
Where silliness has just begun.
In this chalice full of light,
We sip the joy, morning to night.

## Enchantment in Sunny Glades

In glades where sunshine plays the fool,
Rabbits hide in a shady pool.
With every bounce they twist and dive,
Making sunshine come alive.

The flowers toss their heads and sway,
Whispering secrets on this day.
A butterfly with comedy flair,
Lands softly on a daisy's hair.

Nearby a gnome with a cheeky grin,
Juggles acorns, let the fun begin!
He trips and tumbles on the floor,
And laughter echoes evermore.

In sunny glades where merriment blooms,
Nature dances in joyful rooms.
With every giggle and playful cheer,
The spirit of fun stays ever near.

## The Awakening of Nature's Palette

Nature's paints in colors bright,
Splattering joy in morning light.
Each bloom a comedian, it seems,
Flipping petals, living dreams.

Canvases laced with silly hues,
Carrots in suits and dancing snooze.
A flower pranks the bumblebee,
Saying, "Try to tickle me!"

The trees wear hats made of leaves,
Giving shade while humor weaves.
Squirrels hold an acorn feast,
A comedy show with nature's beast.

With a palette full of shades so bold,
Each hue a laughter yet untold.
So join the fun, let's paint the day,
In nature's art, we find our way.

**Vibrant Whispers on a Breeze**

The wind giggles, tickling trees,
With vibrant whispers and playful glee.
Clouds drift by in a lazy race,
While nature wears a whimsical face.

A joke is told by the buzzing flies,
They laugh and dance, oh what a prize!
The petals blush in vibrant hues,
As if they share the funniest news.

The sun peeks out from fluffy puffs,
While critters play and show their stuff.
A tiny frog leaps, jumps with flair,
Declaring, "Life is but a dare!"

So listen close to breezes laugh,
Nature's humor, a delightful craft.
In every rustle, cheer and whine,
A vibrant joke, in every line.

## Sun-Kissed Echoes of Youth

In fields where laughter floats high,
A butterfly winks as it zooms by.
We chase the sun with giggles and glee,
While the grass tickles our toes, oh so free.

Socks mismatched, we dance to the breeze,
With ice cream dripping, smiles come with ease.
Running in circles, we trip on our feet,
Yet every tumble tastes just like sweet.

Mom's old sunglasses perched on our nose,
We play hide and seek with garden hose.
Daring each other to jump in the mud,
Our squeals of delight create quite a thud.

So here's to the days of unfiltered fun,
With slingshot peas and a laughably run.
The sun-kissed echoes of youth we will keep,
In hearts full of joy, where never sleep.

## Yellow Hearts in Morning Mist

A cackle erupts in the dawn's soft glow,
Sneaking past neighbors with a giggling row.
They might see us there, with dew in our hair,
Waving at squirrels as if they might care.

We sip on our juice, pretending it's tea,
While planning great heists of the cookies we see.
We race through the mist, our spirits take flight,
Each yellow heart shining, a mischievous sight.

Hopping through puddles, we splash and we laugh,
Making grand plans with a chalk-covered calf.
In this foggy morning, all worries just cease,
As laughter transforms into pure, silly peace.

So raise your glass high, no matter how small,
To mischief and fun, let's savor it all.
In the morning mist, we are silly and bold,
With hearts wrapped in yellow, just let it unfold.

## Dreams in a Meadow of Light

In meadows where whimsy gives butterflies flight,
We twirl like the petals, our hearts pure and light.
Wearing crowns of wildflowers, our heads full of cheer,
Imagining giants and spuds that dance here.

We share our wild dreams, silly tales come alive,
Of talking to daisies, how they would connive.
Beneath sunny skies, we spin stories anew,
In our meadow of nonsense, absurdly askew.

Every blade of grass knows our secrets and jokes,
As we play with the clouds, beneath lounging folks.
With bubbles of laughter and dainty delight,
Our dreams wave like ribbons, all fanciful bright.

So let's gather the glow of those whimsical days,
Where laughter and dreams swirl in playful arrays.
In this meadow of light, we'll always belong,
With hearts full of giggles, our bond will be strong.

## Elegy of the Bright Blooms

In a garden of giggles, the bright blooms all sway,
Comrades in colors, we cheerfully play.
With bees doing ballet amongst petals of cheer,
We crown our fine moments in laughter we steer.

Oh, what's this? A flower giving a frown?
We nudge it along, "Stop wearing a crown!"
We'll paint you in sunshine and sprinkle with glee,
And dance 'til the moonlight shines down on we.

Every tussle of petals, a silly old blur,
As gardens bear witness to all that occurs.
No elegy needed for blossoms in jest,
For laughter's their bloom, and they're truly blessed.

So here's to the gaffes, where mischief breaks free,
In a world of bright blooms, it's just you and me.
We'll laugh in the garden, let worries be few,
An elegy joyful, in nature's bright hue.

## Whispers of Spring's Awakening

In gardens lush with glee,
The flowers hum a tune,
While bees do ballet leaps,
And squirrels wear hats, a boon.

The sun pops up like toast,
And birds, they crack a joke,
With butterflies in tow,
They dance and laugh, no smoke.

The breezes tickle grass,
As rabbits play charades,
In this world of silly fun,
Where laughter never fades.

## In the Wake of Golden Blooms

Bees hold a comic show,
They buzz in quirky rows,
While flowers join the cast,
In silly petal clothes.

The daisies wink and nod,
As tulips stand on guard,
With giggles in their stalks,
They make it quite the yard.

A cat perched on a fence,
Is plotting with a mouse,
To steal the nectar tea,
And hold a garden house.

## A Tapestry of Yellow Petals

The sun spills laughter bright,
On petals soft and bold,
With yellow smiles that sway,
In stories yet untold.

A merry band of ants,
Parade in tiny shoes,
They march beneath the skies,
Chasing the morning blues.

A breeze whispers a riddle,
To flowers in a row,
The punchline makes them giggle,
As they sway to and fro.

## Beneath the Sunlit Canopy

Underneath the wide blue,
The petals play their part,
A comedy of colors,
That tickles every heart.

The clouds toss popcorn skies,
As laughter fills the air,
With every blooming face,
A joyous daffy dare.

A dandelion bursts forth,
Like confetti on the ground,
And all the blooms erupt,
In giggles all around.

**Sunshine Wrapped in Petals**

Petals dance in the warm breeze,
Wearing sunshine like a hat,
Bees laugh as they find their tease,
While butterflies do acrobat!

Rooted dreams in a flower bed,
Make the squirrels break into cheer,
Whispering secrets, so well spread,
Even worms want a front-row seat here!

Bumblebees buzzing, what a show,
Hosting parties with nectar flow,
The tulips are stealing the glow,
"Who knew blooms could steal the show?"

In this garden, fun knows no bound,
Fluffy clouds join in on the sound,
As laughter lingers all around,
In sunshine's embrace, joy is found.

## Serenade of the Blossoming

Swinging blooms sing silly tunes,
The daisies lead the parade,
Hummingbirds bring in the boons,
While the sun glows, unafraid.

Petal parties start to rise,
Marigolds lead the conga line,
Roses throw in a few surprise,
"Can you keep up? We're feeling fine!"

With a wink, the tulips sway,
All the flora dance and tease,
Nature's rhythm leads the way,
A funky bloom brigade, if you please!

When evening falls, they bow in glee,
"See you next spring, come join the spree!"
In gardens filled with jubilee,
Nature's laugh, a symphony.

**The Language of Golden Stems**

Joyful petals engage in chat,
With bees acting as the mailmen,
Flowers pass notes, 'What's up with that?'
"Did you see the antics of Ken?"

Sun-soaked laughter for all to share,
In the garden, joy's on repeat,
Each bloom a friend, a buddy to care,
Spilling secrets beneath their feet.

"Nobody wears yellow like me,"
Cried a sunflower with great pride,
"This sunny hat is quite the key!"
While tulips roll their eyes, then hide.

In this vibrant floral hub,
Life bursts forth with joyful zest,
Golden stems and nature's club,
Where every petal feels the best.

## Echoes of Joyful Gardens

In gardens lush, giggles erupt,
As petals giggle, swirl, and spin,
Dancing around, they're highly cupped,
Chasing critters as they begin.

Sunlit blooms play hide-and-seek,
With shadows dancing all around,
Peeking through with laughter sleek,
Nature's joy in leaps abound.

"Did you see that bee take a dive?"
A tulip chuckled, oh what fun!
With sunny smiles, the blooms connive,
To throw a bash for everyone.

When dusk arrives, the giggles hum,
"Tomorrow brings more fun," they say,
In gardens where joy's never numb,
Blossoms blended in playful play.

## Golden Light and Gentle Breezes

In fields of yellow, bees take flight,
Chasing laughter, oh what a sight!
The sun is grinning, clouds retreat,
This golden charm is quite the treat.

A squirrel dances, with acorn in tow,
It twirls in circles, putting on a show!
The flowers chuckle, sway to the beat,
Oh, how nature makes life so sweet!

A butterfly lands on a nosy croc,
It flutters by, what a funny mock!
They giggle and tease, in the warm sun's glow,
Taking selfies, in nature's row.

When evening sunsets, all spark and hue,
Fireflies blink, a zany crew!
With each little spark, a wink in the air,
Nature's humor is everywhere!

## A Dance of Harvested Whimsy

In the garden, gnomes take a chance,
Wobbling awkwardly in a silly dance.
The tulips giggle, in friendly jest,
As the sun warms up for its daily quest.

The carrots parade, dressed all in green,
With jackets of dirt, they're a funny scene.
Radishes roll, so round and bold,
In this whimsical tale, so bright and gold.

A tiny frog hops on a big green leaf,
Singing out loud, beyond belief!
His friends all join, making quite the sound,
In this jovial patch, joy abounds.

As night descends, stars start to peek,
The crickets chirp, it's their turn to speak.
With laughter still lingering, the garden sighs,
A dance of whimsy beneath the skies.

## Petal Soft on Lively Days

Beneath a sky of cotton candy hues,
Butterflies whirl, in their fanciful shoes.
The flowers sway, with a giggle or two,
As the breeze whispers secrets, bright and new.

A ladybug dons a polka-dot hat,
Exploring the garden, cheeky and sprat.
With each tiny step, the petals laugh loud,
At the colorful antics of this vibrant crowd.

Sunshine spills laughter, over each bloom,
Creating a stage, for joy to consume.
The petals join in, with chuckles and cheer,
Celebrating life, as springtime draws near.

As shadows stretch long, day takes its bow,
The daisies sway, and whispers allow.
In gardens of humor, the fun never frays,
Petal soft moments fill lively days!

## Spring's Serenade of Gold

In the cradle of spring, where joys unfold,
Nature hums tunes, both funny and bold.
The daisies and bees, in a whimsical play,
Crafting a serenade, brightening the day.

A chipmunk juggles seeds, quite bravely so,
While the tulips nod, in a comical show.
The sun's warm smile makes everyone sing,
Even the clouds can't resist joining in.

The breeze tells tales of mischief and jest,
As petals react with giggles, no less.
A parade of colors, all lively and gay,
In this golden season, let laughter sway.

As twilight arrives with a wink and a sigh,
Fireflies buzz softly, lighting the sky.
In the rhythm of spring, joy glimmers bright,
With a serenade of gold, through day and night!

## The Allure of Verdant Dreams

In fields of green, things get wild,
Petals dance, like a playful child.
Butterflies giggle, they zoom and sway,
Chasing the sunlight, come out to play.

Bees wear tiny hats, buzzing with glee,
Forming a band for the blooms, you see.
With every twist and every turn,
Nature's circus awaits, it's our turn!

Frogs in the pond, croaking a tune,
Geese waddle by, displaying their swoon.
Each plant has a secret, a joke or two,
Join in the laughter, it's all up to you!

So gather the blooms and raise a cheer,
Nature's comedy show is finally here.
In this green world, let your worries drift,
With each funny flower, you'll find a gift.

## Sunshine's Embrace in the Meadow

Sunshine spills like syrup, sweet,
Ants march along in tiny feet.
Hopping from flower to flower, they say,
'Look at us, we've got all day!'

The breeze tickles petals, they giggle and sway,
Saying, 'Who needs plans? Let's just stay!'
Ladybugs gossip on green leaf chairs,
Spreading rumors of the sky and flares.

Clouds float by, tales all their own,
One claims it's made of soft ice cream cone.
'Catch some drops,' they whisper and float,
While daisies dance like they just won a vote!

So if ever you're down, just come take a peek,
Amidst laughter and blooms, you'll find what you seek.
A meadow of joy, a patchwork of cheer,
Promises of laughter, come gather near!

## Threads of Gold in the Landscape

In gardens of glitter, golden rays shine,
Worms in tuxedos say, 'Isn't this fine?'
Styled in the soil, they strut with flair,
Who knew these critters had such great care?

The sunflowers stand, tall, proud in line,
Winking at each other, feeling divine.
One tips its hat, the other goes 'Wow!',
'You're the king of the patch, take a bow!'

Giggling blades of grass join the fun,
Stretching out legs, planning a run.
With each burst of laughter, the butterflies spin,
A carnival moment, let the games begin!

So wander these fields, this land decked in gold,
Where even the critters have stories to be told.
For in every bloom, there's a chuckle or two,
In this patch of delight, there's always room for you!

## Awakening Memories in Bloom

Pastel petals whisper of cheer,
Reminding us once, laughter was near.
A squirrel on a branch, cracking jokes down,
Makes every passerby ponder with a frown.

'Hey there, friend, what's your dream?' it calls,
While tulips giggle in their colorful halls.
The breeze plays pranks, it swirls and twirls,
Knocking off hats from posh little girls.

Each bud a story, a knock-knock surprise,
'Why did the bloom cross the road?' with bright eyes.
'To show its colors, so bold and bright,
In the arena of nature, it steals the spotlight!'

So remember this laughter when times seem dim,
Each bloom holds a secret, let the joy swim.
In a world full of quirks, your heart will find bloom,
Awakening memories, banishing gloom!

# **A Rustic Ode to Golden Fields**

In fields of gold, the cows do prance,
With flowers that waggle in a happy dance.
Their laughter bubbles like a brook,
While bees wear shades, oh, how they look!

The tractors hum a silly tune,
Chasing clouds across the afternoon.
The corn whispers jokes in the breeze,
As squirrels debate on who to tease.

Sunshine plays peekaboo with cows,
While chickens draft their gossip vows.
Each stalk of wheat has a tale to spin,
In this golden world, we all fit in!

So raise a glass to the fields so bright,
Where laughter blooms like stars at night.
With every tickle from the breeze,
We find our joy among the leaves!

## Splashes of Color in Gentle Shadows

In a patch of color, bunnies roam,
Painting daisies in their home.
With brushes made of whiskers fine,
They smear the grass with laughter divine!

Butterflies dance, a circus afloat,
While ants engage in a tiny boat.
They rule the world with silly flair,
In shades of pink and polka-dot air!

A gopher's hat made of a daisy crown,
He struts like a king, but tumbles down.
With giggles shared beneath the sun,
Every flower knows the game of fun!

So wink at the blossoms, give them a spin,
And join the mischief, let the fun begin.
In nature's palette, let joy collide,
As colors and chuckles take a wild ride!

## **Meadow Songs of Radiant Mornings**

When morning breaks, the meadow sings,
With chirps and flutters of all sorts of things.
A rooster's call, a squirrel's laugh,
Nature's band in its silly half!

The daisies gossip, the clovers tease,
As they tickle the soft morning breeze.
With wiggles and giggles, they take the stage,
Creating laughter from page to page!

A hedgehog waddles with style and grace,
Trying hard to win the flower race.
But oh what a sight when he trips and rolls,
Under the giggling gaze of moles!

So let us dance with the morning light,
As meadow songs take to the flight.
In every step, let joy be found,
In nature's laughter, we are unbound!

## The Secret Life of Lisping Blooms

Behind closed petals, secrets spill,
With lisping blooms that share a thrill.
They whisper tales of bees and sun,
Of cheeky pests who dare to run!

Lilies strut with a genteel air,
While tulips giggle, without a care.
They plot and scheme, oh what a fuss,
Deciding who shall ride the bus!

Roses debate about their perfume,
While violets blush in their bloom.
Pansies wear masks for a funny show,
Hiding their truths from those who don't know!

So listen close to the blooming crew,
For nature's jokes are shared so true.
In every petal, there's laughter wrapped,
In the secret life, we're all entrapped!

## The Flourish of Radiant Blooms

In a garden where the flowers dance,
A bee lost its way, took a chance.
It buzzed and it spun, oh what a sight,
Wearing pollen like a suit, feeling bright.

Crickets chirp, adding to the play,
While worms host a wiggly cabaret.
Each petal's a laugh, each leaf a grin,
Nature's party, let the fun begin!

The blooms are in colors, a silly parade,
Roses wear hats that they never made.
Sunflowers wobble to a cheeky beat,
As butterflies dance on their dainty feet.

With each tiny raindrop that falls from above,
The flowers all giggle, sharing their love.
In this hilarious bloom, the joy is supreme,
We frolic together in the garden of dreams.

## Mellow Sunbeams and Petal Whirls

Sunshine spills laughter across the ground,
While daisies perform, twirling round.
They bump into bees, which give them a nudge,
"Hey, watch out!" the clumsy buds grudge.

A squirrel in shades joins the vibrant scene,
While tulips gossip and soil looks keen.
The breeze tells a joke, carries it far,
A plant feels a tickle from a passing car.

Petals flutter down like confetti bright,
As butterflies swoop, what a marvelous sight!
They gossip and giggle about the nearby bugs,
In the silly sunlight, giving out hugs.

Each stem is a joke, each leaf a fun pun,
Painting landscapes where laughs never shun.
In this world of color, joy takes its twirl,
A merriment carnival, oh, what a whirl!

## The Glow of Life in Greenery

Underneath a big oak, the critters convene,
With acorns as cups, they toast to the green.
Squirrels bring snacks, and they giggle with glee,
As grasshoppers dance, jumpy and free.

A turtle in shades takes it slow,
While rabbits perform a hopping show.
With nature's orchestra, the chorus of cheer,
Even the shy toads now join here.

Sunshine glints off puddles, reflective and bright,
Where dragonflies tease, making quick flight.
"Quack!" said the duck, with a wink in her eye,
"Hurry up, party's starting, don't be shy!"

With each little rustle, the laughter extends,
In twirls and turns, as the sunlight descends.
Life blooms in the greenery, fun at its core,
A symphony of giggles that we all can explore!

## Nature's Canvas of Golden Shimmers

Fields splash colors like a painter's spree,
With flowers in bloom, dancing wild and free.
Pansies wear smiles, whilst tulips partake,
In a giggling canvas, more laughs to make.

Each breeze tells a story, tickles the air,
While bunnies jump high, without any care.
Sunbeams peek down, spreading mischief anew,
As blossoms shake hands with a bright, merry hue.

The daisies are chatting, exchanging their tales,
Of funniest moments when wind makes them flail.
Clover leaves chuckle at a ladybug's race,
In a game of hide and seek, each finds their place.

Nature's own show in a riot of glee,
Where laughter and colors dance endlessly.
In this glittery meadow where joy sings aloud,
We twirl with delight, oh how we are proud!

www.ingramcontent.com/pod-product-compliance
Lightning Source LLC
Chambersburg PA
CBHW071820160426
43209CB00003B/146